Thrilling Tarantulas

by Peter Murray

sundance™

Sundance Publishing
33 Boston Post Road West
Suite 400
Marlborough, MA 01752
800-343-8204
www.sundancepub.com

Adapted from *Naturebooks,* published in 2003 by The Child's World®, Inc.
P.O. Box 326
Chanhassen, MN 55317-0326

Photo Credits: Front cover, pp. 9, 10, 21, 25, 26, 29 © Robert and
Linda Mitchell; p. 2 © Gary Vestal/The Image Bank; p. 6 © Willie Holdman/
Index Stock Imagery, Inc.; p. 13 © J. Mitchell,O.S.F./Animals Animals;
back cover, p. 14 © Rhys A. Brigida; pp. 17, 18, 22 © Brian Kenney; p. 30
© Mitch Diamond/Index Stock Imagery, Inc.

ISBN 978-0-7608-9348-7

Printed by Nordica International Ltd.
Manufactured in Guangzhou, China
June, 2011
Nordica Job#: CA21100649
Sundance/Newbridge PO#: 226616

Contents

1 Meet the Tarantula!

You are walking in the **desert.** Before you is a small hole in the ground. You wonder what lives there. A mouse? A lizard? You sit down and wait. After a long time, you see movement. A hairy leg reaches out. It's as long as your finger. One by one, more legs reach out. You count eight legs in all. Then you see a body. It is fat, fuzzy, and brown.

It's a tarantula!

This desert tarantula is moving over a rocky patch of ground.

Tarantulas are spiders. They have eight legs and eight eyes. Their body has two parts. The head and chest are in the front part. This area is called the **cephalothorax.**

The back part is called the **abdomen.** It is the area where their silk is made. But they don't use their silk for webs. They use it for their nests.

This is a female Mexican bloodleg tarantula.

Tarantulas have **venom,** or poison. It comes out of their **fangs.** They use it to kill the insects and animals they eat.

Usually their venom is not dangerous to people. Being bitten by most tarantulas is like being stung by a bee. It hurts at first. But then it goes away.

Here you can see a drop of venom on the fangs of this king baboon tarantula.

3 Are There Different Kinds?

There are about **800** kinds of tarantulas. They live in warm places. They are found in Mexico, South America, and the southwestern United States. They also live in Africa, Australia, and India. Most live in the ground in holes called burrows. Others live in trees.

Most tarantulas can fit in your hand. But the goliath birdeating spider is too large for that. It's almost as big as a **dinner plate!** It eats birds, bats, and frogs. It even eats snakes.

Put your hand up to the picture. A goliath birdeating spider is really this big!

Tarantulas can't actually see very well. Instead, they use leglike **feelers** called **pedipalps** to tell where they are going. Tarantulas also move slowly. So how do they catch their dinner?

Tarantulas hunt at night. **In the dark,** they are able to avoid their enemies. They can search for their food without being bothered.

This goliath birdeater is pulling a baby bird to its mouth with its pedipalps.

I think I'm going to croak!

To hunt, a tarantula first finds a hiding place. Then it **waits for its prey.** Staying very still, the tarantula can feel the **vibrations,** or movements, around it. With any luck, the prey will walk close by. When it does, the tarantula runs toward it. The tarantula lifts its body and pushes its fangs into the prey. Then it shoots out some venom. The prey dies. And the tarantula enjoys its meal.

This cobalt blue birdeater tarantula has attacked a grasshopper.

First the tarantula shoots a special liquid into its prey. This liquid make the prey's insides **soft.** Next the tarantula picks up the prey. It holds the prey against its mouth. Then it slowly sucks out the prey's *juices!*

A tarantula might kill even if it's not hungry. It **wraps the prey** in silk. Then it brings it back to its burrow. Now the tarantula has food for later.

This Colombian brown tarantula is feeding on a grasshopper.

19

In the fall, tarantulas mate. After mating, the male quickly **crawls away.** He knows not to stay around. The female might eat him!

Soon the female is ready to lay her eggs. She **spins a web** on the floor of her burrow. There she lays hundreds of eggs. The female wraps the eggs into a **ball of silk.** Then she works hard to protect this **egg sac.** On cool nights, she even keeps it warm with her body.

Main Photo: This curlyhair tarantula is laying her eggs.

Inset: An ornamental tarantula is guarding her egg sac.

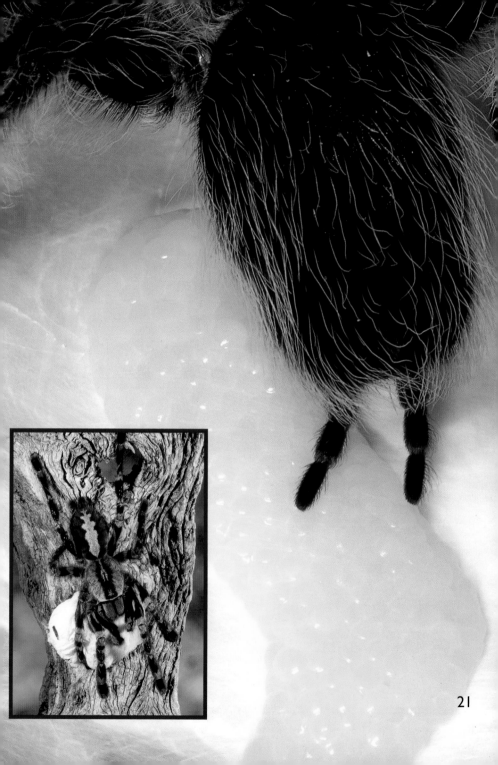

The eggs hatch after about six weeks. A few days later, the baby tarantulas leave their mother. They look for hiding places of their own. This is the most dangerous time of their life. Lizards, snakes, birds, and other tarantulas like to eat them. If they survive, they can live as long as 25 years!

Here you can see baby Brazilian salmon pink tarantulas.

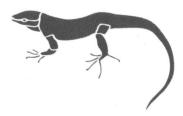

A tarantula does not have bones. It has skin that is hard, like a **shell.** This shell is called an **exoskeleton.** As a baby grows, it gets too big for its exoskeleton. So it sheds the old skin, or **molts.** A new skin waits under the old one.

The new exoskeleton is soft. It **stretches,** too. The tarantula stays somewhere safe until the skin **hardens.** A tarantula will molt many times. It can even grow back a leg!

Can you see the old skin of this molting tarantula? It's below the arrow in this picture.

The tarantula hawk wasp is a different kind of enemy. The female uses the tarantula as **live food** for her baby. First she lands near a burrow. She waits for the tarantula to come out. Then she injects it with **venom.** The tarantula is unable to move.

The wasp pulls the tarantula down into a hole. She lays an egg on top of it. Then she fills the hole with dirt. In a few days, a baby wasp hatches. This **wormlike larva** is hungry. So it slowly eats the tarantula alive!

A tarantula hawk wasp
is capturing this tarantula.

A tarantula has fangs that look very **fierce.** It might show them if it is cornered. It hopes the enemy will get scared. Sometimes it strikes out with its fangs. But most of the time, a tarantula simply **runs and hides.**

Some tarantulas try something else. With their back legs, they break off hairs from their abdomen. The **hairs float** through the air. Then they get into the eyes and skin of the enemy. These hairs are irritating!

Main Photo: This tarantula is raising his legs to appear larger.

Inset: This tarantula has a bare patch where it kicked off its hairs.

Many people have tarantulas for pets. Is that a surprise? You must be **gentle** if you get one. Don't let it crawl on you. It could easily fall! A fall to the floor could kill it.

Pet tarantulas should live in a **terrarium.** This is a large glass cage. It should have everything that a wild tarantula would have. That means water, live food, and a hiding place. You might never want a pet tarantula. But you can still appreciate these **beautiful spiders.**

This girl is carefully touching a pet tarantula.

Glossary

abdomen the back part of a spider's body; contains organs that make silk

cephalothorax the front part of a spider's body; contains eyes, mouth, fangs, stomach

egg sac a baglike holder some animals make to keep their eggs safe

exoskeleton a shell-like skin that covers a spider's body

molts sheds the outer layer of skin, fur, or feathers

pedipalps leglike feelers a spider uses for feeling its way around and holding things

terrarium a container for raising animals or plants

venom poison that some animals make in their bodies

vibrations rapid movements

Index